W9-BLV-380

ideals
VALENTINE

Vol. 49, No. 1

Publisher, Patricia A. Pingry
Associate Editor, D. Fran Morley
Art Director, Patrick McRae
Contributing Editors, Marty Sowder Brooks, Lansing Christman, Deana Deck, Russ Flint, Pamela Kennedy, Nancy Skarmeas, John Slobodnik
Editorial Assistant, Kristie L. Wilkins

ISBN 0-8249-1096-6

IDEALS—Vol. 49, No. 1 February MCMXCII IDEALS (ISSN 0019-137X) is published eight times a year: February, March, May, June, August, September, November, December by IDEALS PUBLISHING CORPO-RATION, P.O. Box 148000, Nashville, Tenn. 37214. Second-class postage paid at Nashville, Tennessee, and additional mailing offices. Copyright © MCMXCII by IDE-ALS PUBLISHING CORPORATION. All rights reserved. Title IDEALS registered U.S. Patent Office. Printed and bound in the United States. POSTMASTER: Send address changes to Ideals, Post Office Box 148000, Nashville, Tenn. 37214-8000.

SINGLE ISSUE—$4.95
ONE-YEAR SUBSCRIPTION—eight consecutive issues as published—$19.95
TWO-YEAR SUBSCRIPTION—sixteen consecutive issues as published—$35.95
Outside U.S.A., add $6.00 per subscription year for postage and handling.

A VALENTINE by Grace Noll Crowell: Used by permission of the author's estate. COULDN'T LIVE WITHOUT YOU from WHEN DAY IS DONE by Edgar A. Guest, copyright 1921 by The Reilly and Lee Company: Used by permission of the author's estate. KIDS IN SNOW SUITS and SKATING POND by Edna Jaques: Used by permission of the author's estate. FOR THE COMING OF SPRING, from the book THE PRAYERS OF PETER MARSHALL, edited by Catherine Marshall, copyright © 1949, 1950, 1951, 1954 by Catherine Marshall. Published by Chosen Books, Fleming H. Revell Company. Used by permission. Excerpt from STILLMEADOW ROAD by Gladys Taber. Copyright 1962 © by Gladys Taber. Copyright renewed 1990 by Constance Taber Colby. Reprinted by permission of Brandt & Brandt Literary Agents, Inc. Our Sincere Thanks to the following whose addresses we were unable to locate: Juanita Johnson for GARDEN WONDERLAND; Ruth Wilson Kelsey for MY MOTHER'S VALENTINE; C.M. Matson for PROMISE OF SPRING; Elizabeth McMasters Brockway for WHAT MAKES A HOME; Florence Van Fleet Lyman for CANDLE GLOW; and Dor Woods for THE WARM HEART.

Four-color separations by Rayson Films, Inc., Waukesha, Wisconsin

Printing by The Banta Company, Menasha, Wisconsin
Printed on Weyerhauser Cougar

The paper used in this publication meets the minimum requirements of American National Standard for Information Sciences—Permanence of Paper for Printed Library Materials, ANSI Z39.48-1984.

Unsolicited manuscripts will not be returned without a self-addressed stamped envelope.

Inside Covers
Gerald Koser, Photographer

Winter Dawn

Elisabeth Weaver Winstead

Across the sunrise sky I see
In blazing colors drawn,
The grandeur of winter's graceful art,
The ice-crystal world at dawn.

Rainbow colors tier on tier
Across the heavens spread,
Soft coral and pale yellow blend
With lavender, gold, and red.

The sun is etched in radiant light
To stand in dazzling view,
As colors fade and slowly form
A sky of luminous blue.

My captured heart is filled with joy,
When on this wintry morn,
Emblazoned in beauty, past all belief
Dawn's winter jewel is born.

Photo Opposite
WINTER MORNING
Conway, New Hampshire
Fred Sieb, Photographer

FEMALE CARDINAL
Adam Jones, Photographer

A Winter Gift

Deborah George Hyland

Deep within the winter gray
There flashed a bit of red;
And where there once was gloominess,
A cardinal stood instead.

He perched upon the feeder's edge,
Standing straight and stout;
A brisk wind stirred his feathers up
And snowflakes swirled about.

4

MALE CARDINAL
Adam Jones, Photographer

His gentle chirping made a song
That soothed the air until
He settled in to eat some seeds,
Content, despite the chill.

This tiny, crimson focal point
Recast the snowy scene,
Transforming winter's barren view
From dismal to serene.

He seemed to share a secret
By his calm within the squall;
If he could brave this season's chill,
Then so could one and all.

He stayed his time, then flew away.
And as he left I knew . . .
God sent this cardinal gift today
For me, and now for you.

The Waiting Time

Garnett Ann Schultz

Winter isn't only cold
Nor only snow and ice;
Winter has so many things
So very dear and nice.
It isn't just the nippy air
Or frost upon the pane;
Winter is a treasured time
To thrill our heart again.

Winter isn't only depths
Of whiteness everywhere,
Nor is it just the frozen earth,
The fields so lone and bare,
The little brook so quiet now,
The birds that do not sing;
And yet the winter holds a charm,
A true and wondrous thing.

Winter is the prophecy
Of warmth that soon shall be,
The promise of the springtime sun,
A budding April tree,
A hush, a solitude, we know,
A dream of joys to come;
Winter is the waiting time
Before the springtime sun.

6

Photo Opposite
OLD BRICK HOUSE
Frederica, Delaware
W. Talarowski, H. Armstrong Roberts, Inc.

BLESSINGS MANIFOLD

Mildred Spires Jacobs

The frozen beauty of God's world
With trees bowed down by snow,
Reveals in all its pristine charm
The peace we long to know.

And knowledge that the spring will come
To rescue earth from cold,
Gives faith that His eternal love
Brings blessings manifold.

Photo Opposite
FROST ON NEEDLES
North Cascade Mountains, Washington
Ed Cooper, Photographer

Skating Pond

Edna Jaques

They dart about like water bugs
With waving arms and sprawling legs,
Some of them graceful as a swan,
And others stiff as wooden pegs,
And yet the fun they have is worth
More than the minted gold of earth.

The ice is clear as painted glass,
Bordered by heaps of drifted snow,
The winter sky above the trees
Almost as blue as indigo,
A setting lovely as a gem
Set in a vacant lot for them.

They swoop and dip and whirl and dart
Fall with a thud and slide a bit
Crawl on all four like tiny bears
Yet never seem to tire of it,
But up and at it once again
Crusted with snow like frozen men.

Their little cheeks are warm and red
Like apples on the rosy side.
Snow suits of red and green and blue,
The little bodies tucked inside
Are warm as kittens wrapped in wool
Lovely to look at . . . beautiful.

Here on this vacant lot is heard
Young laughter merry as a lark,
The gay voice of a little girl,
A tiny dog's excited bark,
Where all the bells of heaven chime
Under the spell of wintertime.

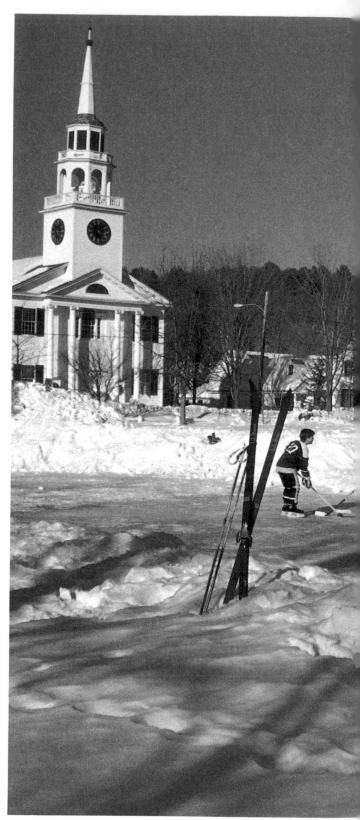

SKATING
Norwich, Vermont
Hanson Carroll/FPG

10

Dog in the Snow

Catherine E. Berry

He ran across the porch as usual,
But when he plunged into
  the soft, wet snow,
He stopped so suddenly,
  one small foot raised
Above the white expanse.
He did not know which way to turn
  for all about him lay the first snowfall
  that he had ever seen.

With little ears in pointed peaks
He took a careful step or two
  where once had been the patterned walk
That led to friendly trees,
So distant now,
  so lost beyond the gate;
He leaped back to the porch
  and shook himself,
Deciding, wisely,
  he would rather wait.

"MAX," PUREBRED SIBERIAN HUSKIE
Barry L. Runk/Grant Heilman Photography

DOG IN SNOW
C. Vladimir Pcholkin/FPG

Kids in Snow Suits

Edna Jaques

They look for all the world like little elves,
Who have invaded our dull universe,
You'd think an artist caught them unaware,
To illustrate a bit of playful verse.

A dozen colors mock the rainbow's tints
Scarlet and hunter's green . . .
  a coat of blue,
A little hood framing a gentle face,
That smiles a lovely smile in passing you.

Together hand in hand they walk along,
Like little cardboard dolls in stiff array,
Or goblins from a far enchanted land,
Given a little while on earth to play.

A red poke-bonnet tops a bobbing head,
And lo a tiny miracle takes place,
Behold a child is turned into an elf
With flaxen curls to frame a pixie's face.

This morning when the world
  was misty white,
I saw them passing gayly hand in hand,
My heart stood still in wonderment and joy,
For this poor common street was Fairyland.

A Child to Love

Garnett Ann Schultz

You can have your wealth and riches
All the things so many seek,
Position, power, fine success,
The fame you long to keep.
You can earn so much you wish for,
Reach a status high above,
But none of these can equal
Having one sweet child to love.

'Tis the greatest gift from heaven,
Little arms that hold you tight,
And a kiss so soft and gentle
When you tuck them in at night.
A million precious questions
And each story often read,
Two eyes so bright and smiling,
And a darling tousled head.

God can never match the goodness
Of a trusting little face,
Or a heart so full of laughter
Spreading sunshine every place.
A child to hold and cuddle,
'Tis a gift from God above,
And the world is so much brighter
When you have a child to love.

Photo Opposite
BE MINE
Obrien & Mayor/FPG

Daddy's Little Valentine

Garnett Ann Schultz

You're Daddy's little angel
As precious as can be,
Not very big, that's certain
But all the world to me.
I love you, little darling,
I'm very glad you're mine,
So once again, I tell you
You're Daddy's Valentine.

You're Daddy's little lassie,
A big important part
Of every new tomorrow;
You've stolen Daddy's heart.
No one could ever doubt it;
You're all that's dear and fine.
A treasured little sweetheart—
You're Daddy's Valentine.

How very fast you're growing,
So soon the time will come
When someone else will steal the heart
Of Daddy's precious one.
Give him your love, my Darling,
But promise through all time
That I shall always rate a kiss
From Daddy's Valentine.

In Daddy's Footprints

Georgia B. Adams

Walking in Daddy's footprints through
The newly fallen snow,
Oh, what delight to span each step,
And laughing as I go.

Oh, his prints are great and manly;
They look like a giant's tread!
But Daddy says they're not that big—
It's just the way they spread.

Sinking way up above my knees,
The going gets quite hard,
For here and there I miss a step
And his perfect pattern's marred.

But oh! It's fun to follow Dad
Through newly fallen snow;
Oh, what delight to span each step
And laughing as I go!

God Made
My Heart a Valentine

Minnie Klemme

God made my heart a valentine;
Inscribed it with His light divine.
He filled it with some lovely things:
The early songbirds in the spring,
The snowflakes and the wayside flowers,
The golden moments, golden hours.

He added yet sincerity,
And hope and faith and charity,
And love and mirth and mischief too,
And made my valentine for you.

Photo Opposite
TEA AND TOAST
William Johnson, Photographer

THROUGH MY WINDOW

Pamela Kennedy

I am not sure a woman ever quite forgets her first love. There is something so vivid and clear about it that, even years later, the heart beats faster at the remembrance of it.

I first fell in love at an early age. He was tall and broad in the shoulders. His hair was the color of a raven's wing and his eyes the clear, pale blue of forget-me-nots. He would have laughed at that description, embarrassed by its naked sentimentality, but it is a true description, nonetheless. His was an easy smile, quick with a joke or a humorous remark, and he had an unending repertoire of silly songs, ready to be sung with just a little coaxing.

His songs were the key to his heart. He sang them to me and patiently taught me the words and melodies until I had mastered every verse. Then he and I would sing them together everywhere we went. They were camp songs and barbershop tunes, raucous choruses, and love songs that tore at your heart. We sang them all. And I would rest my head against his muscled arm and

things old and well-made. He knew the secret; love looks with the eye of the beloved and not with the cool assessment of an accountant, tabulating value in dollars and cents.

He was generous too with his emotions. His arms were always open as was his heart. Some men would have thought it weak to shed a tear; not he. Not often, but every now and then, a beautiful melody, a loving look, a fear, a shared heartache would reach from inside and well up in his eyes. He could be touched by life and I loved him for it.

We parted many years ago. I had the need to move on, to seek new loves, new experiences, to try my wings away from his protective and safe, familiar arms. And in his wisdom, he knew that to hold me back would only kill the love we shared. I was younger then; I didn't think how it might have hurt him. I was too consumed with me.

So he released me, blessed me, wished me well and I never turned to see his tears. I only looked ahead. He knew it would be different. I didn't have time to consider changes then. I marched off, confident in myself and in the knowledge that if I failed, his love would always catch me.

Now, decades have passed since I first fell in love with him. His hair is silver, but his eyes still shine in forget-me-not blue. His smile still comes with ease and often he sings the songs we used to love. There is much that has not changed in all these years, but also much that has. I have fallen into another love, deep and lasting, spanning half my life. My days are filled with children of my own and homes in far off places.

But we still talk and write and even see each other now and then. And there is nothing that will ever replace that first and endless love we share. Daddy, you'll always be my valentine.

Pamela Kennedy is a freelance writer of short stories, articles, essays, and children's books. Married to a naval officer and mother of three children, she has made her home on both U.S. coasts and in Hawaii and currently resides in Washington, D.C. She draws her material from her own experiences and memories, adding bits of imagination to create a story or mood.

smell the scent of him and love him more.

He was a giver of gifts. Not extravagant ones all the time, but special things that showed he knew what mattered most to me. They were never given with strings attached, but handed over with abandon from the overflow of his affection. He gave valentines all year long, not just in winter's chill, and they were more appreciated for coming unexpectedly.

There were silly things like an antique saw handle, that someone else would have thought an awful gift, but I loved it. He had found it in an abandoned garage and I was touched that in the dusty cobwebs of a summer afternoon's wanderings, he had thought of me and my delight in all

She Walks in Beauty

Lord Byron

She walks in beauty like the night
  Of cloudless climes and starry skies;
And all that's best of dark and bright
  Meets in her aspect and her eyes:
Thus mellow'd to that tender light
  Which heaven to gaudy day denies.

One shade the more, one ray the less,
  Had half impair'd the nameless grace
Which waves in every raven tress,
  Or softly lightens o'er her face—
Where thoughts serenely sweet express
  How pure, how dear their dwelling-place.

And on that cheek, and o'er that brow,
  So soft, so calm, yet eloquent,
The smiles that win, the tints that glow,
  But tell of days in goodness spent,
A mind at peace with all below,
  A heart whose love is innocent.

TRAVELER'S Diary

Nancy J. Skarmeas

Niagara Falls

Put the words romance and travel together in the typical American mind and more often than not the result is Niagara Falls. Whether we have been there or not, we harbor a vision of the place—the Honeymoon Capital of the World, the site where countless American marriages make their start. Yet, despite their traditional connection, romance and Niagara Falls are not on the surface a logical pair. What is romantic, after all, about water plummeting into a 190 foot gorge at a rate of 700,000 gallons per second?

Scientists estimate that Niagara Falls, actually three separate falls, are between 10,000 and 30,000 years old. The Falls are a part of the Niagara River, which flows out of Lake Erie into Lake Ontario. The first Europeans to lay eyes upon the Falls were French traders and missionaries exploring west from their settlements along the St. Lawrence River in the early seventeenth century. For the next century and a half, the area passed from French to British and finally, after the War of 1812, to American possession.

The falls at Niagara—the world's seventh natural wonder—quickly became America's first tourist trap. By 1850, new rail systems put the Falls within a night's travel from the large northeastern cities; suddenly, everyone who had read or heard about the great American natural wonder was making plans to see it first hand. Unfortunately, many visitors discovered less of the natural and more of the man-made wonder. Capitalists and con men, seeking to make their living off the Falls, lay in wait for unsuspecting visitors, charging them unreasonable fees to ride in their coaches, stay in their hotels, shop in their souvenir stores, and eat in their restaurants. Some even advertised guided trips to the bottom of the falls and, after collecting one fee at the top, demanded a second fee to guide visitors back up again.

The influx of tourists created a captive audience, not just for the Falls' rushing waters, but for a group of daredevils who discovered their own way to cash in on Niagara. Led by a French tightrope walker named Blondin, these bravely self-promoting men crossed the falls on ropes without nets, walked the rushing currents on giant stilts, and plummeted through the cascade into the gorge in barrels and homemade shells, all to the delight of the assembled tourists and the benefit of their own fame and finances.

Daredevils, con men, and tourists weren't the only regulars at Niagara; the Falls became a requisite stop on the tours of the rich, powerful, and famous. The guest list from the second half of the nineteenth century includes Abraham Lincoln, Charles Dickens, Walt Whitman, and the Prince of Wales. Nathaniel Hawthorne traveled to Niagara and was so overcome by the anticipation of seeing the Falls that on his first approach he reported himself unable to look upon the wonder, afraid it could not match his expectations and afraid that if it did, he was unworthy of considering the sight. Such literary hyperbole did little to discourage the influx of tourists and little to encourage appreciation of the Falls on a basic, natural level. The world's seventh wonder had become a great American sideshow.

The combination of natural spectacle and cultural oddity at the Falls developed a powerful grip on the American imagination, and thus, the "Honeymoon Capital of the World" was born. It was more adventurous curiosity, it seems, than romantic idealism that turned Niagara into a favorite honeymoon spot. Given the opportunity to take a vacation, working Americans flocked to Niagara, both to see what all the fuss was about and to share in the excitement.

In 1885, the future of Niagara was altered by an agreement between the United States and Canada to convert the area surrounding the Falls into protected parks; with great foresight, the two governments promised to put an end to the human circus and preserve the natural wonder. Gone were the tightrope walkers and con men; eventually, the area resumed its natural appearance. And while an occasional daredevil does slip by and the souvenir shops are still active and plentiful, the attraction today is the Falls themselves, unenhanced by human spectacle.

The hype that turned Niagara into America's first tourist trap and earned it the nickname "Honeymoon Capital of the World" has subsided, but Niagara is forever fixed in the American mind as a place for romantic getaways. This is fortunate for those travelers who still choose to make the Niagara tradition a part of their own experience. There is still a healthy tourist trade at Niagara, but today it is intensely focused on the Falls as a natural wonder. Visitors can look up at the Falls from a cruise ship on the river below or from the crashing cascade on a guided, soaking, walking tour. Helicopter rides provide a unique perspective on the precipice, as do the peaceful islands in the river above the Falls. There are still beautiful hotels and elegant restaurants and all the other amenities that define a successful tourist attraction, but Niagara is no longer a trap for tourists; the Falls draw visitors today and the Falls do not disappoint.

Each night at the Falls, however, a bit of the old spectacle does return, when the natural wonder is bathed in man-made light to allow for after-dark viewing. But this is a perfect balance of natural wonder and human promotion and it creates an atmosphere worthy of both the designation of seventh natural wonder and of honeymoon capital; for in the presence of the great rushing falls, one of the most awesome natural sights in the world, the rest of the world shrinks away and the combination of romance and Niagara seems entirely natural.

A Little Valentine

A little valentine came to say,
"I wish you a happy day."
It features a teddy bear getting the mail
From a box fastened to the porch guard rail.

A rainbow brightly arches the sky,
With billowing clouds rolling by.
A promise of blue skies here to stay.
All symbols of a perfect day.

Crystal Krohn
Wausau, Wisconsin

Valentine Wishes

Valentines are in the stores;
  In the windows, on the door;
Smoochy cards with words so sweet,
  Even some that you can eat.
Lacy cards, shaped like hearts,
  Crazy cards with moving parts;
But I don't care about food or sonnet,
  I just want one with
My name on it!

Thais Williams
Salt Lake City, Utah

Reflections

Homemade Valentines

The kind of valentines you buy
May be of fluted lace,
Or have a lovely satin heart
With ribbon bows in place.
They may be sweetly scented
With a sachet-like perfume,
So real you need not close your eyes
To see a rose in bloom.

But oh, the ones I treasure most
Are neither sold nor bought,
But made from scraps of paper
And trimmed with loving thought.

There may be finger smudges
In the center of the heart,
But a little child is cupid
Who scrawled the tiny dart.

But the valentine is precious,
If you look in eyes of blue
And he points to staggered letters
That spell out, "I love you."

Mildred Perl Van Horn
Monroeville, Indiana

MY MOTHER'S VALENTINE

Ruth Wilson Kelsey

My mother has a treasure box
She sometimes lets me see.
Inside there is a valentine
As lovely as can be.

It is an old, old valentine.
Its shape is like a heart.
A cupid hides among the flowers
And holds a tiny dart.

I love to touch the valentine;
I open it with care.
Then Mother reads the little verse
That we see written there.

The verse says, "Dear, I love you."
And that is true, I know;
For Daddy gave the valentine
To Mother long ago.

SIXTY VALENTINES

Mary J. Kellar

He handed her some chocolates
And a card for Valentine's.
With a voice so soft and gentle,
He whispered, "Are you mine?"

Her golden hair had turned to gray,
Her eyes were still dark blue.
She handed him a special card,
And answered, "I love you."

Years could not change this tenderness,
That love brought to their souls.
Through sixty years, through sixty cards,
Their precious love was told.

Through sixty years their love had grown,
Tender moments were entwined,
They'd always love, they'd always be
Each other's valentine.

from
The Stillmeadow Road

Gladys Taber

Valentine's Day is a sentimental, beribboned and flowery holiday. It is a time to say "I love you" with roses and violets and heart-shaped cakes. And I have said before, and will repeat, that it is not a time to send funny valentines which are neither funny nor suitable. Those who wish to make a joke of Valentine's Day are insensitive as well as ignorant. After all, it is a saint's day, a romantic day. It is for the delicate joy of first love. It is also for an expression of lasting love. Even my father, who didn't believe in foolishness, always gave Mama a potted plant on Valentine's Day, usually a cyclamen.

When I was very young, we made our own valentines with colored paper, paper lace, cut-out roses and bluebirds and violets. Like May baskets, the donor was supposed to be a secret. "Guess Who." But after Mama died, I found a packet of valentines in a drawer labeled "Gladys made these herself."

Later, when I acquired my first beau, I hoarded my twenty-five cents a week until I had enough to buy him a book of poetry, which I fear was Laurence Hope's *Song of India*. Father never increased my allowance for special occasions because he did not wish me to become a spendthrift. So a lot of banana splits and hot fudge sundaes went into that book.

I now believe Father was right, although not for his reason. But sacrifice for your first love is a blessed thing and adds value to the gift.

A Valentine

Grace Noll Crowell

I found an old, old valentine
Of my mother's yesterday;
An age-stained, lacy, lovely thing
That she had put away
Between the covers of a book;
And as I touched it there,
I saw her young and beautiful,
The sunlight on her hair,
The love-light in her dark, young eyes
That years could not destroy;
And through the paper lace there walked
My father as a boy.

Somewhere along the heavenly lanes
Today, their eyes ashine,
I think he asks her once again
To be his valentine.

Photo Opposite
ANTIQUE VALENTINE
Superstock, Inc.

Valentine Greeting.

BITS & PIECES

I will make you brooches and toys for your delight
Of bird song at morning and starshine at night.
I will make a palace fit for you and me,
    Of green days in forests
    And blue days at sea.

                      Robert Louis Stevenson

I could never explain why I love
anybody, or anything.

                  Walt Whitman

Love . . . is like a beautiful flower
   which I may not touch,
   but whose fragrance
   makes the garden
   a place of delight just the same.

          Helen Keller

If you would be loved,
love and be lovable.

        Benjamin Franklin

The sense of the world is short—
Long and various the report,—
  To love and be beloved;
Men and gods have not outlearned it;
And, how oft soe'er they've turned it,
  'Tis not to be improved.

Ralph Waldo Emerson

Love gives itself;
  it is not bought.

Henry Wadsworth Longfellow

Love sought is good,
  but given unsought is better.

William Shakespeare

First love is an instinct—at once a
gift and a sacrifice. Every other is a
philosophy—a bargain.

A. S. Hardy

Love possesses not
  nor would it be possessed;
For love is sufficient unto love.

Kahil Gibran

Thus let me hold thee to my heart,
  And every care resign:
And we shall never, never part,
  My life—my all that's mine!

Oliver Goldsmith

39

from
Song of Solomon

Rise up, my love, my fair one,
and come away.
For, lo, the winter is past,
the rain is over and gone;
The flowers appear on the earth;
the time of the singing of birds is come,
and the voice of the turtle
is heard in our land. . . .

Arise, my love, my fair one,
and come away.

O my dove . . . let me see thy countenance,
let me hear thy voice;
For sweet is thy voice,
and thy countenance is comely.

Song of Solomon 2: 10-14

Photo Opposite
VALENTINE FLOWERS
N. McFarland/FPG

THE WARM HEART

Dor Woods

It is the warm heart
That truly makes the home,
Reaching forth with love
Encircling its own.

It is the warm heart
That opens wide the door,
Reaching those outside
Who knew not love before.

WHAT MAKES A HOME

Elizabeth McMasters Brokway

'Tis the fire's soft warm welcome
And the daylight's mellow glow,
Friendly books and easy chairs,
And the folks we like to know.

The love and light and laughter
That go singing through the gloam,
And telling us of peace within,
That makes a home a home.

Candle Glow

Florence Van Fleet Lyman

When night comes down to softly dim
  The mellow sunlight in the room,
I draw the curtains and keep out
  The shadow and the gloom.

I light the candles and the glow
  Steals o'er the supper board and all
The ruddy hearth-fire flaming bright
  Lights up the floor and wall.

For all within a home should be
  Sacred to family life and way,
Safeguarded from the world outside
  When ends the busy day.

Not open to the public gaze
  Through unlatched door or pane,
But hid away for near and dear
  At candle glow again.

A SLICE OF LIFE

Edgar A. Guest

Couldn't Live Without You

You're just a little fellow
  with a lot of funny ways,
Just three-foot-six of mischief
  set with eyes that fairly blaze;
You're always up to something
  with those busy hands o' yours,

And you leave a trail o' ruin
  on the walls an' on the doors,
An' I wonder, as I watch you,
  and your curious tricks I see,
Whatever is the reason
  that you mean so much to me.

You're just a chubby rascal
  with a grin upon your face,
Just seven years o' gladness,
  an' a hard and trying case;
You think the world's your playground,
  an' in all you say an' do
You fancy everybody ought to bow
  an' scrape to you;
Dull care's a thing you laugh at
  just as though 'twill never be,
So I wonder, little fellow,
  why you mean so much to me.

Now your face is smeared with candy
  or perhaps it's only dirt,
An' its really most alarming
  how you tear your little shirt;
but I have to smile upon you,
  an' with all your wilful ways,
I'm certain that I need you
  'round about me all my days;
Yes, I've got to have you with me,
  for somehow it's come to be
That I couldn't live without you,
  for you're all the world to me.

Edgar A. Guest began his illustrious career in 1895 at the age of fourteen when his work first appeared in the Detroit Free Press. *His column was syndicated in over 300 newspapers, and he became known as "The Poet of the People."*

HOME INDEED

Douglas Malloch

Draw up a chair, and light a light,
  And find a book to read.
The heavens are dark, and wild the night,
  And home is home indeed.
The louder seems the Winter's ire
Tonight, the brighter seems the fire,
  For, when the wintry storms begin,
  The more the comfort here within.

The wind is at the window-pane,
  The wind is at the door;
It shakes the house, and shakes in vain,
  For loud the chimney's roar,
And higher leaps the crimson blaze
In Winter than in Summer days,
  The more the weather is unkind,
  A greater joy we find.

The fields in Springtime call us forth
  Their rosy paths to roam,
But when the wind is in the north
  We pluck the rose at home.
Perhaps God sends the wintry hours
To show that there are other flow'rs,
  For, when a roof and fire you need,
  Ah, then a home is home indeed.

Photo Opposite
VICTORIAN SITTING ROOM
Jessie Walker, Photographer

LEGENDARY AMERICANS

Nancy J. Skarmeas

Milton Hershey

Chocolate, the classic Valentine's Day gift, is an American passion throughout the year. We consume it at the rate of three and a half pounds per person, per year, and U.S. factories produce twenty-one percent of the one and a half million tons of chocolate made in the world each year. Even our government recognizes the value of the chocolate bar. Each of our soldiers during World War II received something known as U.S. Army Field Ration "D"—a four-ounce chocolate bar. More recently, during Operation Desert Storm, our soldiers were given HERSHEY'S DESERT BAR™ chocolate bars.

For this national obsession, we must thank Milton Snavely Hershey. Mr. Hershey, the founder of America's largest chocolate factory, did not invent milk chocolate, but he almost singlehandedly transformed it from an expensive specialty confection into the world's most popular sweet indulgence.

Milton Hershey did not set out to make his living producing milk chocolate; after a childhood of poverty, he began his career eager to make a successful living. He entered the world of candy making rather by chance after a moment of clumsiness got him fired from his first job as an apprentice at a Lancaster, Pennsylvania, newspaper. From that moment on, however, Mr. Hershey was devoted to his new trade, sticking with it even after a string of disappointments and failures that left him penniless well into his thirties.

Following his short-lived venture in the newspaper business, Mr. Hershey served an apprenticeship in candy making near his home in Pennsylvania. His first solo venture was an attempt to sell caramels in Philadelphia during the city's centennial celebration. When that failed, Mr. Hershey packed up and moved on, setting up shop in Denver, Chicago, New York, and New Orleans. Success proved elusive, however, and Mr. Hershey returned home to Pennsylvania in 1886 too poor even to ship with him his few belongings.

Home for Mr. Hershey was Pennsylvania's Derry Church, the heart of one of America's richest dairy regions. Born in 1857, Mr. Hershey grew up surrounded by rolling green fields dotted by grazing cows. When he returned to the area not much had changed, except his perspective. A veteran—if not a very successful—candy maker, Mr. Hershey took a second look at the landscape surrounding him and began for the first time to realize the potential hidden among the green pastures and grazing cows of his home place.

To understand what Milton Hershey saw in the pastures of Derry Church, we must understand a little about the state of candy making at the time. Chocolate had, for centuries after its discovery, been consumed only in liquid form. The first solid eating chocolate was sold in England in the middle of the nineteenth century. Solid chocolate was immediately popular, but it remained relatively uncommon because of the expense and difficulty of production. Milk was a central ingredient, but in the days before refrigerated transport, fresh milk was not always easy to come by in great volume. Chocolate, dependent upon fresh and abundant milk for both quality and quantity, could not become a universal favorite until the problem of the milk supply was solved.

Milton Hershey, then, was the right man, in the right place, at the right time. Once he had become convinced through his years of experience that fresh milk was indispensable to good candy, and once he had made the connection between this need and the abundance of fresh, local milk in south central Pennsylvania, the future of milk chocolate was in his hands.

His fist venture after his return to Pennsylvania was not chocolate making, however, but a caramel he called HERSHEY'S CRYSTAL A which, like chocolate, depended upon fresh milk. Mr. Hershey made his caramels in a small shop in Lancaster, daily bringing in milk from the outlying farms. The caramels were a huge success, and within a few years, Mr. Hershey had gone from penniless wanderer to one of Lancaster's wealthiest and most respected citizens.

But Mr. Hershey was not satisfied. For a long time, he had believed that milk chocolate had the potential to be the world's favorite candy. Mr. Hershey began experimenting with chocolate recipes and methods of production. Once his caramel business had proven the value of the local milk supply to good candy, Mr. Hershey decided to go one step further. He sold the caramel business and made plans for a chocolate factory outside the city, in the heart of dairy country.

Mr. Hershey had developed, in his years of hard work and little reward, a powerful, single-minded determination to succeed. Once he had decided to make chocolate, and to make it in a factory surrounded by dairy farms, no amount of good-intentioned advice to the contrary could deter him. With a million dollars made from the sale of the caramel business, Mr. Hershey built what would one day be America's largest chocolate factory—in the middle of country roads and cow pastures. He equipped it with advanced German chocolate-making machinery that he had observed and purchased at the Colombian Exposition in Chicago, and he set himself to the task of producing milk chocolate.

Success did not come overnight. Mr. Hershey worked long hours perfecting his milk chocolate recipe and adapting and expanding the German-made machinery for mass-production. When his recipe was refined to his satisfaction, he took on the task of developing his products. The ideas for HERSHEY'S® milk chocolate bar, HERSHEY'S® milk chocolate bar with almonds, and HERSHEY'S KISSES® chocolates were said to have been Milton Hershey's own; regardless of their origin, it was his decision to concentrate on these simple candies rather than more expensive confections. And it was this decision that within a few years made Mr. Hershey a millionaire. Milton Hershey had revolutionized the mass-production of milk chocolate and made his own name synonymous with good milk chocolate in America.

Today, Milton Hershey's company is the largest single producer of chocolate in the United States. The small, company town that he founded to provide homes for his workers in the factory's country setting is now a thriving community and a tourist attraction. And sweet, creamy milk chocolate, thanks to the serendipitous combination of one determined man, Pennsylvania dairy country, and the world's sweet tooth, is America's favorite treat, on Valentine's Day and every other day of the year.

51

Hand-Dipped Chocolates

Mildred Brand

To many people, candy and chocolate are synonymous; however, most people have restricted themselves to making simple fudge and have left the more complicated looking hand-dipped chocolates to the professional candy makers. With a few simple instructions, however, hand-dipped chocolates can be in anyone's candy making repertoire. (Chocolate-flavored coatings are easier to work with.) Work on a clear, cool day in a 60 to 70° kitchen free of steam for best results.

Dipping Chocolate

1. The amount of chocolate needed to dip centers will vary. As a general rule, melt one pound chocolate to coat one pound of centers (50 pieces).

2. Heat water to a boil in the bottom of a double boiler (without chocolate near stove).

3. Remove water from heat; place chopped block chocolate-flavor coatings, chips, or wafers in top of double boiler over hot water.

4. Stir occasionally, until chocolate is melted (about 3 to 5 minutes).

5. Remove chocolate from hot water and allow coating to cool for 10 to 20 minutes; or place chocolate over cold water and stir until it thickens slightly.

6. Replace hot water with warm water in bottom of double boiler.

7. When chocolate has thickened slightly, place it over warm water in double boiler and it will be ready to dip. If chocolate is too thick to dip centers, warm water slightly. If chocolate is too thin, replace water with cooler water. Lukewarm water at 98° should keep chocolate-flavored coatings the right temperature for dipping. Important: Do not drop water into chocolate. If you do so, dip the water out with a dry spoon.

8. Keep chocolate stirred while dipping. Let dipped candy cool till firm on waxed paper.

Basic Fondant

Makes about 125 ¾-inch centers

    5   cups sugar
    1   cup whole milk
    1   cup heavy cream
    4   tablespoons butter or margarine
    ½   teaspoon vanilla or almond
         flavoring (optional)
    1   cup chopped nuts (optional)
         Dipping Chocolate

In a large saucepan, combine all ingredients except flavoring and nuts. Stir until sugar is moistened. Place over high heat. Bring to a boil, then gradually lower candy thermometer into boiling syrup. Cook without stirring, lowering the heat slightly as mixture thickens. Cook to 236°. Pour out on a marble slab and cool to lukewarm. Work fondant back and forth with spatula until fondant turns creamy white; then knead with hands until it is very smooth, adding flavoring or chopped nuts, if desired. Form into a ball and let rest on slab until completely cool. Form into ¾-inch balls and dip in chocolate. To store fondant, wrap tightly in waxed paper or plastic wrap, place in a bowl and cover with a damp cloth.

Peppermint Patties

    2   cups Basic Fondant
    ¼   teaspoon peppermint flavoring
         Few drops green food coloring
         Melted semisweet chocolate

Work Basic Fondant until softened. Add peppermint flavoring and food coloring. Form into 1-inch balls and flatten each into patties. Dip in dipping or melted semisweet chocolate.

Orange Pecan Creams

    2   cups Basic Fondant
    ¾   teaspoon orange flavoring
         Few drops orange food coloring
    ½   cup finely chopped nuts
         Dipping Chocolate

Work Basic Fondant until softened. Add orange flavoring, food coloring and chopped nuts. Blend all together. Form into ¾-inch balls and dip in chocolate.

Photo Opposite
HAND-DIPPED CHOCOLATES
Gerald Koser, Photographer

Special Today | Special Today | Special Today | Special Today | Special Today | Special Today | Special Today | Special Today | Special Today | Special Today | Special Today | Special Today
FANCY | TOP ROUND | ROUND | SALT | POT | FRESH PORK | PURE | PORK | SLICED | SMOKED | FRESH | BEEF
FOWL | STEAK | STEAK | PORK | ROAST | SAUSAGES | LARD | CHOPS | BACON | SHOULDERS | EGGS | LIVER
3 | 59 | 45 | 25 | 35 | 49 | 17 | 45 | | | | 35

1942 Grocery Store in Provincetown, Massachusetts   The Bettmann Archive

Housekeeper to Eight Million

Good morning, housewives! Cranberry crops are a little larger than expected, so you can buy them at the same price you paid last year . . . tomatoes, cucumbers, and egg plant are plentiful, but snap beans are scarce. . . .

Good morning, housewives! The orange season has been late in starting, so prices haven't declined as they usually do at this time; remember the tangerine season lasts till March, but the crop is smaller than it has been in the past 10 years, so you must expect higher prices. . . ."

Seven years ago New York housewives picked up their shopping bags and went out in a market fog. Then Frances Foley Gannon, housewife and mother of five, came on the scene as head of the city market "Consumer Division." Today New Yorkers know that while they sleep her scouts have been out surveying the hauls of fish down on Fulton Street, the carloads of vegetables and fruit shipped to the wharves from across the Hudson. What the "market reporters" find out will be relayed through newspapers, food columnists, and over the ether by Mrs. Gannon to prepare both the little lady down on the Lower East Side and her wealthy neighbor's housekeeper on Park Avenue for "best buys."

Down in Washington, at the Department of Agriculture's Consumer division, experts have been watching Frances Foley Gannon teach New York housewives how to budget. Last year agricultural field workers came from the nation's capitol to see just how New York did it. Then, in the face of constantly rising prices and the cry of "the American Home, the nation's second line of defense," the word went forth:

"Look at what New York has done; those 8,000,000 consume 19 percent of of the country's produce and vegetables. If they can save money on their market baskets, so can you with the same sort of consumer's market service. The Government will send its agriculture experts to help you set it up."

Now today—hardly a year later—there's a chain radio "fish market" service that begins way up on the Pacific coast, comes down via Seattle and San Francisco all the way to New Orleans. Dial your radio any morning now and you're likely to learn what the catch was up at Newfoundland yesterday and when the haul will be in the local market, and which of Neptune's favorites you ought to buy.

Down in Greensboro, North Carolina, and out in Cincinnati and Kansas City and up in New England, they're falling into line with "agriculture on the air" on the New York plan, so the housewives can learn the ebb and flow of supplies and plan their marketing accordingly.

Food moves rapidly in New York. . . . Two o'clock in the morning of every market day, except Saturday, scouts from the New York Bureau of Consumers' Service scout the wholesale markets, spotting the arrival of perishable fruits and vegetables. . . .

By 6 o'clock these scouts know accurately the state of the wholesale markets and the supplies that will be in the corner groceries in the morning. Then these reporters go in person to the municipal radio broadcast station. There they hurriedly type out their reports and turn them over to the waiting Mrs. Gannon.

While she is compiling the reports, her aids are collecting news of the supply of meats, butter, and eggs.

Meanwhile, all this news has been absorbed, catalogued, compared, assembled and prepared in a radio script. And promptly at 8:25 every weekday morning, the calm, unhurried, confident voice of the Director of the Bureau of Consumers' Service goes on the air.

Market news reporting for consumers has been bobbing up and down for several years. Now defense has turned it into an urgent need. Offices of the U.S. Agricultural Marketing Service in more than 50 cities are helping housewives put "Mrs. Gannon's plan" into action. What helps the family breadbasket helps America, they say!

Julietta K. Arthur

Originally printed in *The Christian Science Monitor Magazine*, January 24, 1942

55

Art by Russ Flint

The Land of Story Books

Robert Louis Stevenson

At evening when the lamp is lit,
Around the fire my parents sit;
They sit at home and talk and sing,
And do not play at anything.

Now, with my little gun, I crawl
All in the dark along the wall,
And follow round the forest track
Away behind the sofa back.

There, in the night, where none can spy,
All in my hunter's camp I lie,
And play at books that I have read
Till it is time to go to bed.

These are the hills, these are the woods,
These are my starry solitudes;
And there the river by whose brink
The roaring lions come to drink.

I see the others far away
As if in firelit camp they lay,
And I, like to an Indian scout,
Around their party prowled about.

So, when my nurse comes in for me,
Home I return across the sea,
And go to bed with backward looks
At my dear Land of Story Books.

D. Fran Morley

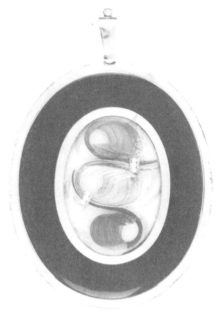

Mrs. Thomas Chase, c. 1803 by British-born artist Robert Field (1769-1819). Watercolor on ivory. Photo courtesy Worcester Art Museum, Worcester, Massachusetts.

Mrs. Thomas Chase. Back of portrait case, showing hair ornament, embellished with gold filigree and seed pearls. Photo courtesy Worcester Art Museum, Worcester, Massachusetts.

Deborah Scollay Melville, c. 1762 by American artist John Singleton Copley (1738-1815). Watercolor on ivory. Photo courtesy Worcester Art Museum, Worcester, Massachusetts.

Precious, Tiny Keepsakes

With their sentimental value and long history, antique miniature portraits can make a unique and heart-warming collection. Made to be worn as jewelry or displayed, miniatures range in size from tiny portraits of the eye, favored by romantic-minded couples in the early 1800s (designed to be secreted away for private viewing only), to larger family portraits (still only three or four inches in height) in elaborate frames or cases.

Miniature portraits have changed with the changing fashions throughout the centuries. They first appeared during the reign of Henry VIII in the early sixteenth century and are believed to have been inspired by portraits on classical coins and carved cameos. The tiny portraits, painted with brilliant, jewel-like colors on vellum, quickly became a royal rage and were originally kept in small "portrait boxes" for private viewing. Soon, the miniatures were set in jewelry and worn as pins, lockets, and bracelets. Enamel portraits on copper were fashionable for awhile, but this style gave way to something more delicate.

By the early eighteenth century, artists in England and Europe developed the technique of using watercolors on ivory. It was a painstaking process, but one that produced portraits with a lovely delicacy and luminosity. The portraits became more detailed even as they shrunk in size, rarely exceeding an inch and a half at this time. It was this type of miniature that eventually found its way to America and became a hit with the early Colonialists who commissioned portraits by traveling European artists. But once again, changing fashions led to a change in style for miniatures.

Perhaps to make room for the high hairstyles of the day, miniatures grew in size to three or four inches, but were still often worn by ladies as elaborate necklaces. An interesting addition to the portraits emerged around this time that also had to do with hair. The portrait painters elaborately wove and braided a lock of the sitter's hair, and decorativly arranged it on the back of the portrait frame. Often the hair was entwined with another's, emphasizing the symbolic, sentimental value of the tiny keepsakes. But like the styles before it, this too gave way to fashion's whim.

Portraits grew larger in size again by the middle of the nineteenth century and became works of art for public viewing, rather than personal mementos. Attention to detail and accuracy increased, producing a smooth finish that mirrored the slick, often cold look of the newly invented daguerreotypes. Unable to compete with the speed and economy of the new photographic portraits, the popularity of miniatures gradually declined and eventually became nothing more than a novelty for the very rich, coming full circle from their beginnings in the Court of King Henry VIII.

While miniature portraits can still occasionally be found today for a reasonable price at estate sales or better flea markets, collectors will have to work hard to find these tiny works of art. Their small size, rarity, and ever-increasing value keep them out of most antique malls, but they can be found in stores dealing in antique jewelry or specialty items from England and Europe. Most of the more valuable, older, or signed portraits are dearly treasured in family collections and are rarely seen for sale.

Your miniatures can be displayed as originally intended—worn as a lovely locket or brooch, or displayed in intimate arrangements on a table-top or wall. Hiding your miniature in a small cabinet or closed box is true to its early personal nature.

It may not be easy to collect a large number of miniature portraits, but even one or two will be rewarding. Because of their highly personal origins, miniatures provide a more intimate connection with the past than is often possible with other antiques. Be certain that the painting you purchase speaks to you; if you are like most collectors, it is likely to be in your family for a long time.

Stephen Salisbury III, 1838 by American artist Eliza Goodridge (1798-1882). Watercolor on ivory. Portrait a gift of Stephen Salisbury III. Photo courtesy Worcester Art Museum, Worcester, Massachusetts.

One of the finest collections of miniature portraits can be found at the Worcester Art Museum in Worcester, Massachusetts. The museum's holdings of over ninety portraits, some of which are shown here, represent more than thirty artists including John Singleton Copley, Gilbert Stuart, James Peale, Robert Fulton, Edward Greene Malbone, and Edward Savage and date from the late eighteenth century through the 1940s. The gallery is the only permanent collection of miniatures in New England.

Rebecca and Debra Hovey, c. 1798 by American artist William Lovett. Watercolor on ivory. Photo courtesy Worcester Art Museum, Worcester, Massachusetts.

CRAFTWORKS

Valentine Portrait Wreath

Marty Sowder Brooks

Materials Needed:

20- or 24-inch grapevine wreath
Burgundy or deep mauve spray paint
18 yards of decorative ribbon
Paper and pencil
Scissors
Two 10- x 13-inch plastic canvas sheets
¼ yard quilt batting
¼ yard deep red velvet or velveteen fabric
¼ yard green silky fabric
¼ yard deep red silky fabric
Craft glue or glue gun
½ yard ruffled eyelet trim
2 yards faux pearl strands
Short lengths of red and white ribbons and trims
1 yard of ¼-inch elastic
Florist's wire
6 mauve or pink ribbon roses
Baby's breath (dried)

Directions:

1. Lay the wreath on a tabletop either outside or in a well-ventilated room and spray with the spray paint until all the twigs are covered. Let dry. Wrap the wreath with 9 yards of the decorative ribbon and secure the ends with glue to the back of the wreath.

2. Using paper, trace one heart of each size from this page. Place the paper heart pattern onto the canvas. Keep the center line of the heart even with the straight lines on the canvas.

3. Cut a heart shape from the centers of several of the large and medium hearts. These will frame your photos, so match the size of the openings to the size of your photographs.

4. Using the canvas hearts as a pattern, cut batting the same size for each heart. Cut and remove the batting from the openings made for each photograph.

5. Place the batting and the canvas hearts on the back of the fabric. Cut the fabric one-half inch larger than the canvas. Trim the opening, leaving a half-inch margin.

6. Clip the fabric around the outside of the heart every ¼ inch and clip directly into the corners and curves of the openings.

7. Put a thin line of glue on the edge of the canvas and pull the clipped edges of the fabric tautly across the sides of the heart. Press it onto the glue and let dry. If necessary, a clothespin can be used to hold the layers together until dry. Repeat this step until all the hearts are covered with batting and fabric.

8. Embellish each heart with trims and beads or stack them for a pleasing look. Fabric puffs, "yo-yos," can be added for interest. To make a yo-yo, cut a circle of fabric four inches in diameter, press under ¼ inch around the edge. Loosely baste around the edge, just inside the fold. Pull the thread tightly and knot. Arrange the gathers evenly on the front of the yo-yo.

9. To attach photographs, for each frame, cut two strips of elastic, one-inch wider than the opening. On the back of each frame, glue the ends of each strip horizontally across the opening. Let dry, then slip the photograph underneath.

10. Position the hearts on the wreath and attach with florist's wire. Glue the solid hearts and yo-yos to the wreath. Fill in between the hearts with the small ribbon roses and baby's breath.

Marty Sowder Brooks demonstrates her crafts weekly on a Nashville, Tennessee, television talk show. She lives in Gallatin, Tennessee, with her husband.

Photo Opposite
VALENTINE WREATH
Ron Little/Rush Photography

M. McCANN

Groundhog Day

Esther Kem Thomas

It's doubtful if a time will come
When folks can truly say

They'd trade one day of sunshine
For one of winter gray!

To be a sunshine pessimist
    Or squint-eyed gloomy Gus
When February skies are clear
    Seems too ridiculous.

I'll take my day of sunshine now
    And chance the weeks to come;

I'll plan, indoors, the lettuce bed
    And fall chrysanthemum.

Oh, I'm anticipating spring
    But, if worse comes to worse,
For six weeks I'll be glad I had
    A taste of sunshine first!

Winter Morning

Margaret Rorke

The sun wakes later but is seen
With greater glory for no green
   (Except the needled pine),
Can shade the eye that fills the east
Or dim its brilliance in the least
   As it looks into mine.

Its glance upon the land I know
Sows glitter on fresh-laden snow;
   Then adds an overlay
Of shadowed patterns as the breeze
Bestirs the barren arms of trees
   To lift a winter day.

Photo Opposite
THE WAYSIDE INN
Sudbury, Massachusetts
Nelson Groffman, Photographer

Country CHRONICLE
— Lansing Christman —

So much is undergoing change in the winter world now that February is here, I never mind the snow and wind and cold that may persist for a few weeks more. It is a time of renewal and it is invigorating. And I believe that I'm not alone in that feeling.

With the sun staying longer on the hills, all of nature is getting in step with the season. It is the light of afternoon, more golden and mellow, that shows the greatest progress. Once the year starts its swing toward spring, the taut, icy fingers of winter begin to relax their hold; you can see it in the swelling buds and hear it in the sweet songs of the birds.

Consider the caw of the crow, so sharp and severe in December now softer and in tune with the season. Listen for the calls and carols of the robins. They've been flocking to the dooryards

66

lately and gathering on warm southern slopes. Their eager beaks search the bare, softening soil for signs of life. The song of the chickadee seems even sweeter this time of year, as does the song sparrow's melody. On bright sunny days you will hear the warble of the bluebird, the bird Thoreau described as "carrying the sky on its back." The birds are eager for spring. They have been inspecting old nesting sites, going in and out of bird boxes on posts and trees in the yard. I can hear the drumming of a woodpecker in the yard and the answer of another drummer in the woods not far away. The birds sense the change in seasons, and so does humankind.

It is appropriate that Valentine's Day comes in the midst of this month of renewal. For the young, it is a time of new beginnings, a time to pledge their everlasting love. We who are older and wiser know that as each new year brings a renewal of spring, so it is for us. We have the opportunity to renew our long-established vows with the promise of love.

The author of two published books, Lansing Christman has been contributing to Ideals *for almost twenty years. Mr. Christman has also been published in several American, foreign, and braille anthologies. He lives in rural South Carolina.*

GARDEN WONDERLAND

Juanita Johnson

My garden is a wonderland
Again when winter comes to call;
A plush white carpet beautifies
The landscape wall to wall.

My barren shrubs are picturesque
With icy branches intertwined;
And often I would like to shout,
"This wonderland is mine!"

A cardinal feeds on scattered crumbs,
His scarlet wings enhance the view;
A snowman stands beside the gate—
His derby hat askew.

A trellis bends beneath the weight
Of flakes reflecting diamond hue;
And for a moment I forget
This was where roses grew.

FOXGLOVE

The Language of Wildflowers

In this month of ice and cold, it's nice to think and talk about spring and the beauty that awaits us in the garden. And as February also is the month of love, what could be more appropriate than a discussion of the romantic language of wildflowers? These bold drifts of many-colored blooms, like love, have a tendency to show up most anywhere; but unlike love, wildflowers require almost no tending to blossom and grow.

To some, wildflowers are just weeds; but the fact is, all of the flowers in our gardens were once simply wildflowers. In another century perhaps, or on another continent, but wild nevertheless.

The Victorians, who seem to have had plenty of time on their hands for such pursuits, created an entire language of romance around the wildflowers which grew profusely in the English countryside. Some of the meanings they assigned to various blooms undoubtedly had their origin in ancient mythology and folklore. The foxglove, for example, is said to have been named by fairies. The fairies gave blossoms to the foxes to wear as gloves, so that they could not rob the henhouse. In the romantic code of the Victorians, foxglove represents "insincerity," perhaps because of the distrustful nature of the fox.

Another myth held that picking the foxglove would offend the fairies. This may have been told to keep the highly poisonous plant out of the hands of children. Foxglove's scientific name, *digitalis*, gives a clue as to its use in heart medicine today, but foxglove can kill if eaten. I would call that insincere!

Another wildflower with a history dating back to ancient mythology is the shy, retiring violet. In ancient Greece, Zeus, in love with Io (the name means violet), hid her from the wrath of his jealous wife by changing her into a white heifer. When she cried—as well she might—he turned her tears into the sweet-smelling, little flowers. The violet was frequently included in Shakespeare's love sonnets to represent humility and constancy in love and was a symbol of modesty and simplicity to the Victorians.

Faithfulness is a favorite theme in the romantic language of wildflowers and several represent this trait. Honeysuckle symbolizes "generous and devoted affection." Heliotrope, a popular wildflower adapted to the garden as long ago as the fifteenth century, has always represented fondness and devotion. The dwarf sunflower represents adoration, as it faithfully turns its face to follow the sun across the sky each day. On the other hand, the majestic giant sunflower does the same thing, but it represents haughtiness!

The meanings assigned to wildflowers often have little to do with their appearance. Sweet William means gallantry and the waterlily represents purity of heart, but the elegant peony is said to represent shame.

Perhaps the most familiar legend in the language of flowers is that of the briar and the wild rose. In ballads, stories, and poems the tale has endured of the faithful, loving heroine abandoned and betrayed by her handsome, ne'er-do-well lover. When she finally pines away and dies of a broken heart, he is so stricken with guilt that he kills himself. From her grave grows the universal symbol of true love, a thornless red rose. From his grows a briar, symbol of remose and lowliness, and the two intertwine for all time. The unfortunate lady might have fared better had she avoided the whole affair and adopted the wild daisy as her symbol. It means, "I'll think on it."

The cold and blustery month of February is a good time to discuss the history, language, and beauty of wildflowers; and you can plan a lively display for your spring garden simply by selecting native wildflowers that are common in your climate and soil conditions. The nicest thing about this type of garden is that the less you tend it, the better it does. Most wildflowers actually prefer soil that is not too rich and not too well-watered and when left alone will bloom, go to seed, and spread about in their own fashion at their own pace.

Like love, a wildflower garden is a constant delight, full of surprises, and always changing. And like love, a wildflower garden will always give you something to talk about.

Deana Deck lives in Nashville, Tennessee, where her garden column is a regular feature in the Tennessean.

Little Crocus

Garnett Ann Schultz

Little crocus in the snow
Fearlessly you rise and grow,
Caring not that winter stays
All along the country ways,
You have courage real and sure
Freezing weather to endure.

Little crocus blooming there
What a precious beauty fair,
Head held high—so brave are you
Hoping spring shall soon shine through,
Treasured beauty—in the sod
Surely from the heart of God.

We admire your tender charms
Still held fast in winter's arms,
Matters not the early date,
Seems that you are never late.
First bright blooms to bring us cheer,
Little crocus—small but dear.

Photo Opposite
EARLY CROCUS
G. Hampfler/H. Armstrong Roberts, Inc.

The Promise of Spring

C.M. Matson

The trees are standing stark and bare,
Their limbs embrace the cold;
The signs of winter everywhere
Are easy to behold.

The mountains stand out in relief,
The air is crystal clear,
The smog and dust are washed away
To clean the atmosphere.

The days are short, the night comes fast,
The cold is like a vise,
But very soon the spring will come
To make things warm and nice.

I'll awaken some fine morning and
Gaze out upon a scene
Of fields ablaze with flowers
In a sea of waving green.

The robins will be singing; sweet
Their plaintive springtime song,
So though it's cold outside today,
The winter won't last long.

Heaven's Composition

Stella Walczak

Hush!
I hear a waterfall,
The breath of spring,
A crocus quaking,
A jonquil waking,
A lily bending.

Now I hear them blending,
In God's never-ending
Symphony.

Photo Opposite
DAFFODILS IN SNOW
Larry Lefever/Grant Heilman Photography

For the Coming of Spring

Peter Marshall

We give Thee thanks for the loveliness of spring
  with its promise of summer.
Bird and blossom seem to tell us
  of the possibility of new life for our own souls.

This spring day speaks to us of beginning again,
  of new beauty that can come
  to reburnish our own barren lives.

O Lord Jesus, may that transformation
  begin in us now as we sit before Thee—
  penitent and expectant.

Amen.

Readers' Forum

I love reading and looking at the pictures in your magazine. Since I also enjoy photography, I am sending some photos that I hoped would be suitable for publishing in Ideals.

Sharon Kraus
Nauvoo, Illinois

Editor's note:
Thank you, Sharon. We think everyone will enjoy your photography. We encourage all our readers to submit pictures of their children, grandchildren, or pets. We will print them as space permits.

Sharon Kraus, Photographer

It seems as though I've grown up with Ideals magazine on the coffee table. I've come to really love your magazine, and I look forward to each new issue!

Over the ten years my mother has received Ideals, my view of your magazine has changed. When I was small, the pictures really got my attention. Now that I'm older, its become an old friend. The beautiful poems have brought both smiles and a mist of tears.

Rachel Robbins, age 16
Pinellas Park, Florida

Editor's note:
Thanks for the kind words! We appreciate our new readers just as much as those who have been with us for years.

Statement of ownership, management, and circulation (Required by 39 U. S. C. 3685), of IDEALS, published eight times a year in February, March, May, June, August, September, November, and December at Nashville, Tennessee, for September 1990. Publisher, Patricia A. Pingry; Editor, Nancy Skarmeas; Managing Editor, as above; Owner, Egmont U. S., Inc., wholly owned subsidiary of The Egmont H. Petersen Foundation, VOGNMAGERGADE 11, 1148 Copenhagen, K, Denmark. The known bondholders, mortgages, and other securities holders owning or holding 1 percent or more of total amount of bonds, mortgages, and other securities are: None. Average no. copies each issue during preceding 12 months: Total no. copies printed (Net Press Run) 228,731. Paid circulation 37,146. Mail subscription 166,166. Total paid circulation 203,312. Free distribution 534. Total distribution 203,846. Actual no. copies of single issue published nearest to filing date: Total no. copies printed (Net Press Run) 177,159. Paid circulation 10,048. Mail subscription 154,015. Total paid circulation 164,063. Free distribution 201. Total distribution 164,264. I certify that the statements made by me above are correct and complete. Rose A. Yates, Vice President, Direct Marketing Systems and Operations.

ideals®
Celebrating Life's Most Treasured Moments